A FINE YELLOW DUST

Laura Apol

MICHIGAN STATE UNIVERSITY PRESS ▪ *East Lansing*

♾ The paper used in this publication meets the minimum requirements
of ANSI/NISO Z39.48-1992 (R 1997) (Permanence of Paper).

Michigan State University Press
East Lansing, Michigan 48823-5245

LIBRARY OF CONGRESS CATALOGING-IN-PUBLICATION DATA
Names: Apol, Laura, 1962– author.
Title: A fine yellow dust / Laura Apol.
Description: East Lansing : Michigan State University Press, [2021]
Identifiers: LCCN 2020054447 | ISBN 978-1-61186-402-1 (paperback ; alk. paper)
| ISBN 978-1-60917-677-8 (PDF) | ISBN 978-1-62895-444-9 (ePub)
| ISBN 978-1-62896-438-7 (Kindle)
Subjects: LCSH: Grief—Poetry. | LCGFT: Poetry.
Classification: LCC PS3601.P64 F56 2021 | DDC 811/.6—dc23
LC record available at https://lccn.loc.gov/2020054447

Book design by Charlie Sharp, Sharp Des!gns, East Lansing, MI
Cover design by Erin Kirk
Cover and interior art Adobe Stock | Юлия Глазкова

Michigan State University Press is a member of the Green Press Initiative and is
committed to developing and encouraging ecologically responsible publishing
practices. For more information about the Green Press Initiative and the use
of recycled paper in book publishing, please visit *www.greenpressinitiative.org*.

Visit Michigan State University Press at *www.msupress.org*

For Hanna
and for Jesse
— always.

. . . song is a part of mourning
as light is a part of the sun.

—AUDRE LORDE

CONTENTS

PREFACE

In 2017, my twenty-six-year-old daughter, Hanna, took her own life on a sunny April afternoon. Like every parent who experiences the death of a child, I was utterly shattered. And like all those who experience the death of someone they love to suicide, my grief was complicated by confusion, shame, anger, and guilt.

In the days and weeks that followed Hanna's death, I began to write. I was no stranger to the therapeutic possibilities in writing; leading writing-for-healing workshops was a regular part of my professional life. Yet, after Hanna's death, I had to discover, for myself and from the inside, how writing can prove a respite from and a repository for emotions that threaten, daily, to overwhelm. I took a year—a living-in-and-into-grief year—and wrote. I am a poet, and my writing took the form of poems.

This collection is the result of that year. The poems represent the changing landscape of those months: what I needed to learn, what I was trying to navigate, how words sometimes facilitated and sometimes got in the way of the journey. The poems do not follow in a straight line; they muddle through dailiness, through seasons, and through traditions that are now forever changed.

An elegy is a song of mourning and sorrow, a lamentation; but it is also a song of love. In these poems, I tried to fuse what was unspeakable with my own poetic craft to create something that could endure in the face of loss. The poems represent my deep grief, but they also connect me to Hanna—to her bright spirit, to a love for her that will never die.

A FINE YELLOW DUST

THE LITTLE MERMAID

—COPENHAGEN, APRIL 23, 2017

Such eyes
   as she studies the water.
In four days, she will trade so much.

She knows how it will be:

  a sword through the body.
  Voice bartered.

  She can never
     return.

Soon, she will be only foam
   on memory's sea.

Oh, daughter—

I would touch your smooth cheek,
stroke your hair. Birth you,
    again and again

  —but for the ocean between us.
But for the rocks.

WHEN IT ALL SEEMS TOO MUCH

—and sometimes it is:
$$\text{the unbearable}$$
$$\text{weight}$$

of the blossom, the ache
of the greening grass. Last week, a lone tulip

shot through the rock garden,
a brown rattler slept in the sun.

I slice oranges
for the orioles. They trill from the trees,
unaware

of what the world will do to us.

Or perhaps they already know.

BIPOLAR

Like you, Daedalus, I made my fledgling ready, mapped
for her the promise of stars, crooned their names in her
sleep; mentioned only in passing the dangers of heat and
water, the risks of too high, too low;

spoke instead of mother eagles, how they teach their
young to fly, transporting them upward, letting them go,
swooping under to catch them as they fall, until the eaglets
take to sky. I wanted it to be true.

But flight is a solitary pursuit. I couldn't carry her aloft,
nor catch, mid-fall. On her own, she felt the lift of wind.
The hugeness of heaven. The dizzying wrinkles of waves.

The interminable plunge to the sea.

ONSRA

In the Boro language of India:
"to love for the last time."

There was still snow. Or maybe
it was rain.
    Mud or sun or wind
or March.
    Yes, it was March.
And she told two stories
that ended the same way—

I am so like my Mama Bear.

And we laughed. I'm sure
we laughed.

Did one of us know even then
how April
    —that cruelest month—
would follow,

and that I would
stand in her closet after, bury
    my face

in the scarf she wore
when we hugged
            goodbye—

HOMING

Cycling through Holland that spring,
        I watched them:
the mute swans on their nests of sticks,
the coots' floating platforms in the canals,
an egret's roost on a tower.

I remembered someone told me
how a stork lines her nest
            with feathers
                she tears from her breast
until she bleeds.

            Such a cradle—
it doesn't matter if it's true or not.

I was thinking of mothers
            and daughters then—
my own daughter buying her first house,
how I wanted to be there
—paint swatches, curtains, a new set of pans.

Home later that week, it was a robin
carrying dried weeds all morning
            that caught my eye,
and a small nest in the woods
            —a bunting's, perhaps—
that I picked up
            after the wind:

no feathers, no blood; just slender twigs,
strips of bark lined with lichen,
dead grasses,   thistle down.

TOO LATE

Theodore Roethke,

she lives in your town.
She is going to die there.

Stop her.

Find the words to unlock
the duplex door.

Say to her
   O my sister remember the stars the tears the trains
Tell her
   Out of these nothings
   —All beginnings come.

Remind her
   A lively understandable spirit
   Once entertained you.
   It will come again.
   Be still.
   Wait.

Take her small hand.

ON RETURNING FROM HOLLAND,
I FIND A LONE TULIP IN MY GARDEN

the sun	the tulip	the rocks
the tulip	the stream	the daughter
the stream	the April	the snake
the phone call	the rocks	the night sky
the phone call	the police car	the night sky
the morning	the morning	the mourning
the rocks	the tulip	the snake
the tulip	the stem	the April
the morning	the stem	the cutting
that April	the mourning	my daughter

REVISION

In this poem,   I was not
finishing a glass of Malbec at EnVie
when the call came. The police did not
leave a message, and   I did not
call them back. They did not
say *you need to come home*, and
                        I did not
say *is she okay* and when they said *No ma'am she's not*
                        I did not
think she'd created some new drama and roll my eyes.
In this poem, the police did not
go to the wrong address
and tell a friend who told a friend until word got
to me, and
                        I did not

            wail

   as I drove
onto the on-ramp
and along the whole forty-five miles of interstate,
six miles of county road, 1.2 miles of gravel,
and a driveway a third of a mile long. At the house,
                        I did not
get out of the car.   I did not
stand, for one long moment, my back to the officer
walking toward me.   I did not
look at the stars in the late-spring sky, the familiar
sentinel of trees, the small lights in the windows.
                        I did not
take a last deep breath of my sometime-happiness,
                        did not
say *I just want one more moment of this life,
just one more moment*
                    before I turned to hear
what I already knew.

THE FUNERAL DIRECTOR ASKS

one for sorrow two for joy
                    How many
three for a girl four for a boy
                    How many locks
five for silver six for gold
                    How many locks of her hair
seven for a secret never to be told—

How many locks of her hair
                    do you want?

LULLABY

Then
I wrapped the black
box
         in her baptismal
blanket

—fleece, edged
with my grandmother's
crochet—

cradled her
         as before

sang to her
         as before

rocked her and carried her
home.

INSTRUCTIONS FOR THE FRIENDS WHO ARE SORTING MY DAUGHTER'S THINGS THIS AFTERNOON

I want her coats—the new one she got for skiing,
the old one she wore in the yard, the black one she wore
on the photo in the rain—and the green hat and scarf
she knitted in sixth grade. I want the games: Clue,
cribbage, backgammon, Trivial Pursuit. I want Yahtzee
and the Rook cards, too. And any score sheets
with her name at the top. I want the pink hoodie
with the kangaroo, her yoga mat, all the unmatched
earrings she saved. I want her purses and belts,
her viola and her second-hand guitar. I want her
measuring spoons, her ironing board, the photo albums,
her last bottle of shampoo. I want the Birkenstocks
(even the ones with the worn footbeds; especially
the ones with the worn footbeds), her picnic blanket,
and all the yarn. Save her watercolors, her candles,
her great-grandmother's sewing machine, the t-shirts
she had set aside for a quilt, and her tent. I want her
pillow. Her stuffed elephants. Her felt-tipped pens.
The broken lamp she planned to fix, the doorknobs
she replaced but never threw out. Don't give away
her nail polish or her emery boards. Or any of her rings.
I want her hairbrush, the hair still caught in it.
Her toothbrush. Her last morning. I want the sun
in the window. The cats that woke and stretched
beside her. I want her last phone call. *Goddamn*—
all I want—let me have back   13
her choice.

HERS

Grandcats,
she told me when she got them:

a feisty brown tabby, a long-haired
domestic, a tiny Maine coon mix—

and I bought them toys, carriers,
            collars, and trips to the vet,
brushed them while we talked,

laughed over the photos she sent,
            the stories she told.

When the tabby escaped,
I hung signs, searched her neighborhood
for weeks, checked the shelter
            every three days.

Now, a friend delivers them all to me.

Terrified, they explode
            into this new space—
watch me
from the top of the fridge. Eat only
            when I am away.

Did she tell them goodbye?

They used to sleep
            nestled to her.
Here, they curl together, wild-eyed,
forever out of reach.

PATIENT STONE

In Iran, we have a tradition to help with grief. It involves a "patient stone." When your pain is too overwhelming, you wander the fields in search of "your" patient stone. Once you find it, you sit alone and tell it your story. With each word and each sentence your pain is supposed to lessen until you completely unburden yourself. You know you have reached the end when the stone bursts into pieces.

Amir,
I would like to believe
in your patient stone. All afternoon
       I have searched.

I think it is not so much
       that I will find it—
it will find me.

But
there is much
       I do not understand.

How large is a stone
that can manage this work?

Do I visit it, broken?
Do I carry it home?

I will need
       the right stone;
smooth or shattered, it will be mine
for life.

THE FOX

What I thought I had left, I kept finding again
—W. S. MERWIN

Is this how
she now comes to me—
a glimpse of tawny haunches,
dark muzzle and bright eyes?

The last time I saw her,
she had dyed her blond hair red.
It was brass-orange, a shade
she could not abide.

We washed it together,
my fingers pink with lather, the sink
filled with fuchsia suds.

       * * *

Last week, they gave me
five locks of her hair—amber lights,
copper, rose-gold.

I would have held her if she'd let me
that desperate afternoon
—would have soothed her,
my hands ruddied
by blood.

And the fox? It crosses the road,
peers from the ditch. Turns away,
silent and wary—slips
into the merciless
weeds.

FIRST MOTHER'S DAY AFTER HER DEATH

Before dawn, I wake
    from a labyrinth dream—

       she is lost
       at the center
no matter my search.

Who can reach her?

We used to go for mother-daughter
pedicures;

now paper-white trilliums
       bloom where she stood.

All day, I circle
    the space in me
          that was her.

PERSEPHONE

It was spring. She was gathering
flowers.
    He was watching, always
watching:

        Father,
        god
        of Hell

—and then she was gone,

hungry daughter, taking
        not only six seeds
     but full fruit, blood-red clusters

on her tongue.

In the last moment, her hand
steady or shaking, did she think of me?
    Just before, did she—

What dark
exchange,   waking
       where I cannot
           follow.

I search and search, summer
      into fall, into
winter that never ends—

but there will be
       no more vernal visits,
           no startling shoots
    of green.

OF THE HEART

I tell the doctor my heart is broken and I don't
mean the heartbreak of my daughter who in spring put a bullet
through her breast,
I mean the beat inside me that pushes blood
and sometimes catches, or races, like an animal that runs
where it runs, feels what it feels—a wolf or coyote
like the dead coyote on the side of the road,
no blood or wounds but an open mouth, as if there is more
to taste or take in, an animal that will never be tamed, only
trapped in the cage of these ribs
—so the doctor gives me wires that adhere to
my skin, the glue burning holes in my chest, and it records two
weeks of my life
(a drive cross-country to see someone I once
loved; champagne I drink alone to mark the start of
my fifty-fifth year; time with my son, who needs to believe
I still smile; a visit from a niece who could be my daughter
in the fire's light)
until tomorrow, which is my late mother's
birthday, when I will take off the wires, pack up the small black
box, put it all in the mail. It has recorded the skips and echoes,
the breaks and tripping-overs of these weeks—
fourteen days, three hundred hours, my heart
insistent, a cricket in dry grass.

BIRTH MARK

She had a birthmark,
a mottling—*moedervlekken*—

said to be
some wish of the mother forever unmet,
my own luck or longing impressed
in her skin,   my fear imprinted,

touch of St. Mary,
a wound from her past life
—*muttermal*—

      mark   from birth—

I can see it in my mind,
I can see it—but where?
The top of her foot, her cheek, the base
of her throat, her thigh belly shoulder-blade
thumb.

I touched that stain when they gave her to me,
knew her, then, branded
as mine—*modermærke*—

traced it on her infant self:
the outside of her elbow, the back of her neck
—stork bite, angel kiss, devil's claim—

watched it grow,
mystic geometry revealed
by flip-flops, a two-piece, miniskirts, a backless
dress—permanent and permanently
her.

All her life, I saw it,

yet now, it moves—here; no, here; no,
here. Behind the bend in her knee.
Over her heart. Right temple, left temple,
back of her hand—*maternal impression*—

my mark everywhere,
indelible, singular as the whorls
of her fingers,

she, my newborn, my last-born,
my daughter,   my undoing.

BETRAYAL

She arranged in advance
for three friends
        to take them—

one friend for each cat.

I ask after them now,
and the new owners write
        to tell me
                how things are:

a joke
        that the cat
        wakes too early;

a story
        about a catnip mouse
        between the sheets;

pride
        in learning
        to unsnarl a mat

                —their new lives.

DREAM IN WHICH MY DAUGHTER FORGIVES

She first came to me, grown, in a dream of a bear cub
that followed me to town.
                                    I turned for home but the cub
went on.

Waking, I might have remembered the trees
                                    or the light in the trees.
I might have remembered the pitted road, the painted fence,
or my own self, turning.

I might have stayed inside the long walk home.

But I didn't.

It was her too-familiar anger
            —where was the baby bear; how could it be lost—
her demand to direct a search;

then her question: *First, would you give me a hug?*
                                    that carried me into day.

After so long, her wanting to be held. After such absence,
the asking.   I woke with her

still in my arms. Though of course, she was not—
the baby bear
        unfound; the road
                                    empty;   the late morning
                                                blurred with rain.

PROTECTION

—ANGKOR WAT, CAMBODIA, 2016

I sat on the temple floor in a halo of light, head bowed, feet bare. He sat there, too—ochre robes, the bowl between us gold in the sun. How I wanted what he had blessed: a string bracelet, braided in prayer. Like cathedral candles, bloodied knees—mine was an ongoing bargain with God. Protection strand, talisman, charm; once fastened, it cannot be taken away. I put out my wrist; he knotted my heart's desire—my wanting to believe, my one keening plea: *Daughter*. Since then, I have kept what I promised. A year later, those wrist-threads, frayed, remain. Can I sever the cord now? It did not protect her. Just a brutal reminder: *She is not. Never was. Safe.*

SEAGLASS

The incoming tide is relentless. At my feet, white foam, bits of glass worn smooth. I thought she would be okay—she was buying a house. *Hey Mama Bear, I've got it arranged. I'm looking at properties Friday.* The sea's glass is broken and broken and broken and tossed. Brown, green, white, blue, aquamarine. She said she would be okay—*I'm looking at properties Friday*—studied reviews and ordered a Smith & Wesson online. Seaglass, polished by currents. *I've got it arranged.*

I was in Holland. She was buying a house. Did they do a background check? I said I could bring shoes for her from my trip—let me know the size. *It might be too late, but I'm a ten and a half.* She studied reviews, purchased a Smith & Wesson and found homes for her cats. *I'm looking at properties Friday. It might be too late.* Seaglass the size of teeth—the tide holds more than enough. Why didn't she answer my calls? *We can talk later. I've got it arranged.*

She was approved for a mortgage when she bought a Smith & Wesson. Did they do a background check? *I'm a ten and a half. We can talk later. I'm looking at properties Friday.* Impossible currents— I was away; she stayed home from work, wrote a last note in her journal: *this was ridiculously easy. It might be too late.* Why didn't she call? How relentless this thunder of ocean—glass ground to milk teeth, the tide coming in. *We can talk later. Ridiculously easy. I've got it arranged.*

I was away. She left a note, made plans for her cats, phoned her friends to say goodbye. Didn't she tell me she'd be okay? *Arranged easy I'm too-late Friday*—broken glass in the tides. *We can talk later, Mama Bear.*

THE BABY

in the dream might not be my daughter,
    but I like to imagine—

that she will come to me
                first as an infant,
        so we can grow together
                    into our dream-selves;

that again I can hold her
        hard to my chest, comfort her
            when she cries
        —that this time she can let me.

Jogging through the morning streets
        with her stroller

—*faster Mommy, faster; sing Mommy, sing!*—

I will turn left instead of right, or choose
                    a different tune

and she will learn   a different song,
perhaps take in
                a different set of birds.

ECLIPSE

—AUGUST 21, 2017

She was a toddler then—
        the summer I took her

        outdoors at midday,
    warned her not to look up.

Instead we watched
    the sickles
        of sunlight
—bright confetti—
            scattered
beneath the trees.

I stood between her
and the dangerous sky,

reveled in
    the blond ringlets
    at her neck,

    her prattle
    as she tried to catch
    the crescents
    littering the walk.

Today, the solar hole
    burns me
            blind.

How can I resist
this turning toward,

this gazing at
    the sun's dark core?

END OF THE MOTHERLINE

At five, she was too young
for me to give her the word—
Matryoshka.
        Only the idea:
woman inside woman inside
woman inside. The set of nesting dolls
I'd brought home for her was plain—
outlines burned into wood, gold trim.

I touched the outside:
This is great-Grandma. I split
the largest doll; an identical one
inside *and here is Grandma*, who opened
to another *and Mommy.* I pulled
the me-doll apart, revealing
the tiny solid doll at the core:

And this is you—inside Mommy,
inside Grandma, inside great-Grandma.

But she shook her head, took up
the smallest doll. *This is great-Grandma,*
who is part of Grandma—she reassembled—
who is part of Mommy. And all of you
as the largest doll came together
are part of me.

Matryoshka, motherline—

        who can know
which of us was the center,
which the shell; who failed
to protect;
        who would not be held.

FLIGHT

She stormed down the beach
that day

heels kicking up sand,
arms swinging in righteous
rage

and I let her

—let her believe she could
get away. That easily.

Twelve, tanned,
sure of her own story

—all its injustice—

and ahead
a full week in the breaking
waves, stingrays

hidden on the scalloped
ocean floor, venomous
barbs.

I waited her out, shuffled
through the shallows,

watched the shadows

startle at my feet, their fins
resolute as wings.

ELEPHANT EARS

She loved them—

the two glass-blown elephants from my childhood
turned into a collection I bought for her, brought to her:
brass, carved teak, gold-gilt; one made of cloth, one of
jade—each tiny, intact—trunk raised or curled, solid
circles of feet, and ears flapping, like those green heart-
shaped elephant ears in the garden, wide as my
outstretched arms—leaves that still flap, alive, in wind.
Can she hear me now? She packed her

collection, wrapped in newsprint, with such care.
Fragile—Elephants on the box in her script. *Our writing is
so much alike, Mom,* she used to say. I've hung her
elephant print on my bedroom wall, where I'll see it:
Mama and—protected by the Mama's solid front legs,
stroked by her trunk—child. Over the years: she'd hold
her hand up to mine, palm to palm, to see how her
fingers were almost the same as—were longer than—
mine, her elephant ring

too large for me now, elephant earrings, necklace, there
is nothing she will write again and those lovely fingers
loaded that gun, pressed the trigger, the silence ear-
splitting and what, after all, did she know about fragile,
about handle with care?

SHOOTING

star.   She was

SLEEPING BEAUTY

She could fall asleep in a heartbeat, high gear until she dropped. We have a story about napping and airports—something about an orange, a moving walkway, and a window seat. I've forgotten what it was or why it made us laugh and now I'll never know.

I go over the memories, worried they'll disappear; worried, too, I might wear them out. She did yoga on the boulders in the river. We strung lights at Christmas. I helped her hang artwork in each apartment, winter-proofed the windows, organized socks. One holiday, she nodded off playing Hearts.

My sleeping beauty.

But in the fairytale, the princess doesn't die; she merely sleeps, rouses to a world transformed. With her, the palace slumbers too, wakes—as one—to memories, shared: treadle and spindle, the christening curse.

The aging mother, though, does not sleep. Alone, she carries half-told stories with her to the grave—no one to help create the tellings: crescent pose on river rocks, an orange over the Atlantic, winterized windows, or a poster of the Eiffel Tower hung, just so, above the couch.

RIVER OF OBLIVION

> *Now at Lethe's stream they are drinking the waters that quench*
> *man's troubles, the deep draught of oblivion . . . so that . . . with*
> *memory washed out they may revisit the earth above.*
>
> —THE AENEID

Hanna chose the kitten; I chose the name. The wildest tabby in the litter, feral, rippled with stripes—called her *Lethe*. I had just left Hanna's father; there was much to wish to forget.

That kitten drew blood, exiled itself behind the bookshelf, the dryer; tore up the mattress, hid in the box spring. But Hanna at four was a match: fierce squalls as they wrangled, Lethe clawing out of Hanna's determined embrace.

Our new life: Hanna raged at the upending while the cat took to the basement ceiling. *Wild thing.* Years of taming followed as Lethe learned to curl in a lap, sleep by a side. Hanna settled, too— summers, we would swing by moonlight; winters, sled after dark.

I was overseas when Lethe at sixteen had to be put down—tumor ruptured and a night of brutal bleeding. Hanna slept on our bathroom floor with the terrified cat, blood on the tile. At the vet the next day, she soothed Lethe into sleep. Never forgave me for being away.

Then it was Hanna's own rupture, her brutal bleeding—her bathroom tile.

What now is left to remember, who to forgive? *River, watch for her—that is my girl on the shore.* She has drunk from the stream, been ferried to whatever waits on the other side. In her next life, will there be an echo that tugs: a midnight snow, a swing lit by moon,

or a river-striped kitten—some unnamed longing that no longer draws blood?

PRAYER ON OPENING DAY

—NOVEMBER 15, 2017

Today, I bless
the cold relentless rain,

dampening the shotgun blasts
from down the lane, across the open
fields.

Deer season, two white tails
flashing near the edge of sight, a tawny rush
toward daybreak's gunmetal grey,
and *no*—do not, do not

        go

there; today there is no pleasure
in their bounding grace.

These months,
I have learned: the numbed longing
of daughter-without-mother is no match
for mother-without-daughter—

each yearling is thirst; each doe a broken
line.

And so, on opening day, I wish
that when I startle to these shots,
lie rigid-still in this dark
morning, I could aim my grief

at this grim day, my heart recoiling
with each round—

each leaf the stain of blood.

FELO DE SE

—(tr. Latin, felon of himself)
an act of deliberate self-destruction,
in particular, suicide. ·

She was the grenade
          flung into every family
event: the Thanksgiving flu. Christmas
strep throat. New Year's
          cramps

—the one who rescheduled, refused,
          lashed out,   left early.
Say the truth then:
          it was never easy.

But it was never this hard.

In her absence,
she is louder than she ever was,
     and that ferocity of love
makes this year's holidays,
which should float
          smooth on the surface
                    (no unexpected
upheaval, no sudden
          explosion)—

                    did I say explosion?
There is a trigger warning here:

once more,
I am making plans for the season,
                    the calendar merciless
in its march. As always,
          she will be missing,
and *missing*

is a way to fend off
        what I cannot face.

So today I will pretend
she is not dead.

I will book flights for her
     far from family events:

Amsterdam for Thanksgiving,
     Notre-Dame at Christmas,
New Year's Eve in Sydney—

     those fireworks erupting
   over the Harbour Bridge.

FIRST THANKSGIVING WITHOUT HER

We must unlearn the constellations to see the stars.
—JACK GILBERT

I never gave much thought
to the afterlife
                until this road trip,
so like the last one she and I made
a year ago tonight—

you can never step into the same river

of headlights,
    the same travel playlist, the same
Ursa Major North Star meteor shower
nighttime
                        twice.
    And what about snow?

So if on this solitary drive
I look up to a sky

invisible behind clouds

    —are clouds the sky, or just
    a veil obscuring the sky—

how can I have faith
that somewhere
                there is a moon,
slender, curved and brilliant

—a moon I could see, if only
                I believed.

ONLY BONE

Dry needles spark; fallen leaves carry the flame. We rake
in the autumn cool, tip barrowsful onto the blaze. I stoke the fire,
watch the ash, the haze rise—

atoms of pine, of damp oak; seared resin,
motes of maple that catch and shimmer in the afternoon sun.

My grown son watches, too—smoke finding the sky—
and in that moment, we are again each on a side of the cardboard
casket, the room sterile, the light unforgiving.

In Bali, they send with the dead those things they loved,
and so: a small cloth bag of hair snipped from her cats;
pages from her grandfather's Bible; her grandmother's blouse;
a family photo—always, just we three;

a butterfly for her shoulder, its blue-veined wings.

     * * *

The crematorium walls were cool, the only heat raging
out of sight—

my daughter a numbered disc I set inside the chamber
and later received back to know she was mine. All mine—
a box of ash. What about the ring I slipped onto her finger?
I imagine the inscription, white hot: *Namaste.* Only bone
can survive the flame.

Twice each hour I touched the chamber's door,
measuring loss with my palm until the fire was out,
blower stilled. After,

I sat on a bench in the spring afternoon, studied the light. How far
can molecules travel? Will I meet her in the wash of rain, in the river—
each leaf, each needle a trace: the scent of pine,
flecks in a cat's fur, sunlight through smoke.

     * * *

Today, the season's first snowflakes form around dust. I light the wood stove, blister my hand on its doors. Smoke enters the room.   Fiercely   so fiercely   it burns.

GRIEF

The stillness of snow
holds all sound

—the barred owl's flight, shrieks
of the winter hare, an oak tree groaning
in the ravine.

It cradles
the birth cry, cottons the green shoot,
the white rage.

Falling, it fills
                    what was empty

—the only time
I do not weep for her silence.

PEARLS

Just an FYI: The High School is taking donated dresses
for girls who need them for winter formal.
—FACEBOOK POST, DECEMBER 2017

Strapless, black-and-white satin—

with a sequined bodice
and floor-length, ball-gown skirt.

It will fit someone tall,
with long limbs
        and a graceful neck,
shoulder blades like wings.

She should wear her hair
in an up-do, ringlets framing
a heart-shaped face,

full lips, blue eyes, nose
a bit large,

should ask how much liner
is too much,

incandescent—she should be
           incandescent—

should twirl for me
        before she goes out,
borrow a clutch
        from my closet,

wear my pearls.

FIRST CHRISTMAS WITHOUT HER

—CHICHÉN ITZÁ, 2017

I am here.

I am here
        because she no longer is—

and I cannot face another manger.

There is silence in this rubble,
these   crumbling   ruins,
siege of weeds.

I am here

        because each temple was built
        on the temple before—rocks reused,
        history a study in excavation;

        because the sacred pool
        guards
        the bones and ghosts of drought.

Here, the books have all been burned.

Now the only record is light
tracked across ancient skies

—that, and a stone bowl to hold
what is offered:

        love's obsidian knife,
        my still-pulsing heart.

49

WOUND

In the dream,
I am wearing her earring—
a spiral that winds the outer curve
of my ear six times,
five evenly-spaced holes. It stays
with me long after waking,
that dream—a perfect silver scroll.
I remember
when she had it done, how long
it took her to heal. In the shower,
I shampoo with care. I pull on my blouse
cautiously, slant
my hat so my lobe will not tear,
angle the phone to protect the site.
As I write, I reach
up—Judas, Vincent—to finger
it: her corkscrew helix,
my left
ear.

I RENT A ROOM IN VICTORIA

It is always a matter of tense:
I have a daughter. I had
    a daughter.

She loved to draw.

I have run so far
to escape her ghost, but here
    is Freya, someone else's

    daughter,
             the girl-voice
from the rooms above
              bringing down
a picture she's made
          for me.

From a sheaf of papers
she conjures

a blue angel—

    haunted eyes,
    heavy wings,

the sag of her smile
          so impeccably
             drawn.

GESTATION

The last time I counted months
I was waiting
        for her—she, the rhythm
beneath my stretched
skin. An elbow, a heel,

head up, head down—lotus, bridge,
down-dog, mountain,
                warrior.

The last time I counted months
she was moving
        toward me, my body
readying
to push her into the world.

Now I am counting months again.

Today marks as long
for her to pass
        from sight
as it took her to arrive,
gestation reversed,

a telescope
      turned backward on time.
She has grown smaller,   smaller,
until only I know
        her turns, her slides,
           her flips and kicks.

She is once more the secret
I keep
        at my center—
the delicate curve
of spine, the translucent eyelids
           closed.

AS IF

Far from home, on a bridge
that spans a rushing stream,

suddenly she is tiny and near,
and once more we are gathering sticks,

throwing them into the water,
racing to watch them on the other side.

A thin place.

How can it be that she has found me here
and that, with her hand tight in mine,

we are walking together a path
we have never walked before,

across roots and fallen logs, farther
and farther into the rain,

and we walk
as if we had all our lives to do this—

as if we had all our lives.

METAMORPHOSIS

Fact: to become a butterfly, a caterpillar first digests itself.
Fact: disturbing a caterpillar inside its cocoon or chrysalis
risks botching the transformation.

What is this, if not a cliché? I buy tulips
and visit the butterfly garden on my daughter's birthday.
But she is dead, and too soon
petals like wings litter the table. A metaphor—
larva to pupa to wings, but how will I say it? Butterfly
at the cemetery, catching light. Butterfly
on my shoulder as I leave the glassed-in garden.
I keep counting on signs. A luna moth stays
cocooned for five years, lives three days
and what's the point? Maybe that's the poem—
no lasting transformation, just wrinkled wings,
opening-closing, the start of flight or its end.
But I'd like to write something profound
for her birthday, so strike the part about three days,
remember instead how one spring
—long before I knew how this story would end—
I stopped at a butterfly farm when I was crazy
with worry and cliché was my religion:
metamorphosis, a faith in transitions and slow-drying
wings, each knotted pupa a reminder
I couldn't do it for her, couldn't open her
to the sky. *But she was going to be okay.* I could see shade
beneath the thin walls of the chrysalis, umbra
of the *Blue Morpho*—grace, a split in the skin,
emerging. For so long, my useless hands
ached with the wait. Now on the table near the vase,
petals and a fine yellow dust.

HER FATHER

There is danger—
a man behind me, a great sea
ahead,
            and I am running—

danger, water, running
toward a small yellow boat.

I am holding pages
—words and white space—
clean pages, black type

nearing the boat

but I turn around—
face the danger,
it's her father, face

her father, hold out
to him the sheets. Coolly,

he takes
them from me, takes
his scalpel

holds it to the whiteness

of my inner
arm, draws the blade across
my inner
            arm
and furiously   onto the pages

I bleed.

GROOMING

Because we married young, and in the morning-
after light, his hand with a new ring seemed that of a stranger,
the future open, and so unknown. Because when I left him,
he was lonely and learned horses, moved far away, bought
a ranch. Because my daughter loved horses.
Because she was still a child and I didn't understand:
the pony, the phone calls, the jewelry, the high heels.
Because she was his daughter, too. Once, tenderness
moved in me. The tectonics of pity, remorse.
Now, there is only magma hardened to rock.
Because his hands, his hands—

THE BREAKING

1.

She held her silence tight as that long-ago kitten—
the one that bloodied her arm, left her wailing
on the porch.

That kind of silence.

And when she broke it, she still didn't tell me;
the friends told me—the sitter, her brother,
her therapist, the police.

Those days, she was a grenade, truth the pin
neither of us pulled.

2.

There is a poem I cannot write, though I rise daily in darkness
to try. I can write about her sofa, rescued from the curb,
its floral print, sagging seats; her pots and pans and artwork;
how I cleaned each apartment when she moved in,
when she moved out;

I can write about the things I'm worried I'll forget—
the time she buzzed her hair, that nose piercing, her passion
for crêpes, buttered and sugared, and how she sat on the counter
as I cooked, sat on the floor as she ate,
all chatter. One year she wanted a dark blue bedroom
and we painted the entire Thanksgiving break.

I can write those poems.

I can even write her rage, her fury, the wet laundry, that silent
ride home.

3.

The poem I cannot write is about her father
        —keep going now—   her father.
She wouldn't tell me, wouldn't say it, left it
for me to piece together.

        (hidden pages, clues she gave to others)
        —keep writing—

Summers were his,
so many states away; he wouldn't let me see her,
wouldn't let us talk on the phone. She kept his secrets,
his repeated *no one understands me*
like you do

while he painted her toenails, shaved her legs,
—shopping trips to buy lingerie.

Hungry ghost, he grabbed
        the wheel as she drove, forced
                the car onto the shoulder—

it is my house and I will come into your room   *whenever I*
choose.

4.

How can I write what I didn't know,
               what I only learned too late
and second hand?
I want this poem to be spare, lean—
to hot-lava into the unsaid:

the outings. The Jack and coke.
The keys to the car.

But I wasn't there. I cannot imagine,
will not imagine,   every image a rock
through a windshield, shattered.

I have tried for so long
to write this poem—

instead, I do the dishes, feed the dog,
               plant a tree, another
tree, another; feed the dog, hang towels; edge
the grass, feed the dog. Dig another hole—

5.

This is the poem I cannot write, though I have tried
        for a decade,

     and for this year

and for all the days after I got the calls

      from the friend
      .from the sitter
      from her brother
      from her therapist
      from the officer:
          do you know what that bastard did

and no   —and *NO NO NO*—   why didn't I know it

     how could I miss it
             why wouldn't she say it
to me   and
        this is still
           not a poem I can
write—this silence   breaking
    each line
each word   a black hole
    collapsing into   itself.

LAST ENTRY

in my daughter's
turquoise journal, three careful pages,

her own script—
directions for a funeral, ending

And my father should pay.

Of course he jetted in after,
brief and insistent

—I could not stop him:

I said *but no contact.*
The funeral director
said *next of kin.*

He spent an hour, reported
I have seen her; she is at peace,
flew home.

Can I tell the truth now?

This can never be made right
—no columbine redbud ashes full-moon.
No heaven
or angel; no sorry. No now.

THE CRUELEST MONTH

Go now. The ocean is roiling—white sky, foam
on the rocks. I hear my daughter's
                                voice
in the churn. Is she coming toward me or pushing
away, riding farther and farther out to sea?

            This is the shore
where bears come when they rouse, hungry
for spring.
            Go now. I remember my dream, the cub
following, then not   following. How did I fail
to notice?
            There is the gravel path, out
and back;   the birches, gold
        in the light;   the house,
the door, the brass knob, the wood table.

                    I lost her

is not the same as *she is lost.*
Get it right this time. *Go now.*

                It is April again—
the water's edge littered with rocks.
They are beautiful, each more necessary
                        than the last.

ASH WEDNESDAY

At thirty-five, I knelt at the rail
for the first time, Father Alphonse cupping
a vessel of ash. *Dust you are, and to dust*
you shall return. Repent and believe the Gospel.
He made a perfect

petal of cross with his thumb on my brow,
turned to my small daughter beside me
to touch his finger to her forehead,
but I stopped him. No dust.
No ash.

I thought I could keep her
               from it.

Now, more than two decades later, I kneel
alone, her ashes in a black box I have
yet to disturb. Moses told the people
to paint blood on the lintel
so the Angel of Death

would pass by. What if I had let
that priest long ago mark her as mortal,
as not-mine, smudge her with soot?
Perhaps the Angel might have
passed over—

might have entered instead
               some other distant door.

EASTER MORNING

When the wave rises, it is the water;
and when it falls, it is the same water again . . .
—RABINDRANATH TAGORE

The cherry trees are in bloom,
the grass around strewn
with petals that have fallen
in the night. Is this the mystery
of life or of death? I try to believe
in heaven—some days
yes, some no. This morning,

I do. When does water
turn to wave, and wave to sea?
My conversation with her is forever
undone. Don't tell me someday
it will be complete—by then
I will have forgotten what I meant
to say

and what, after all,
                    will it matter?

ONE TURN FROM SILENCE

echo is one turn
from silence, one turn
from never having heard at all
                    —KAREN ENNS

After everyone else left, I was alone
with her, the tiled crematorium
silent, but for the flame and blowers.
I remembered what I had forgotten—
to play the Hallelujah Chorus
before she met the flame. Not because
there was a whit of praise in me,
but because it was what she had looked
forward to, every year—a family sing-along:
holiday carols, Handel the finale.
For the Lord God omnipotent reigneth.

Those early Christmases, she and I shared
a score; I taught her timing, rhythm,
the weaving of parts, until she took off,
strong soprano, finding her own way
as—standing—we heralded with song:
King of Kings, and Lord of Lords.

So, while she burned, I once more
stood,   held the speaker
near the corrugated metal door
—wondered what she might hear,
her molecules ascending.
And He shall reign for ever and ever.

Easter Sunday, eleven months on, I visit
a church in another city. No jubilant morning
for me, but when copies of the Chorus
are handed out, I take one, stand
with the rest. I cannot find my voice.
Yet there, at the end, comes a moment

where grief and doubt
surge without warning into full-throated
longing, into broad-battered hope
—an echo from silence:
                    Hal-le-lu-jah.

WHO SPEAKS WITH ANGELS

Only then did we know. How it felt
to have loved to the end, and then past the very end.
—JENNIFER GROTZ

1.

Years ago, Richard, a mystic
who speaks with angels,
told me it would all be okay—a daughter
made of air and water who had past lives
to work out in the here and now.

After some hard years, she would be
fine—*Mother-daughter issues are fire issues.*
That's what the angels said to him.

> Today, I'm not in the mood for metaphor.
> And it's hard not to find the angels in error.
> By *fire*, did they mean that cardboard casket
> I slid past the metal doors, the button I pressed
> to ignite the flame?

Back then, Richard said that when my daughter
found her way, she would be a force.
She has no intention of going small.

> I think of waves—
> their push to shore, how they knock me down,
> slam me into sand, face scraped, shoulder
> bruised, how every morning I drown
> into the new day.

So much pain, Richard said;
I'd thought he meant my daughter.

2.

Now Richard says my girl is with those angels, encircled by light, receiving
love. *Intensive healing that will take a very long time.*

I'd like to believe this man who speaks with seraphs, but Richard's angels
get it right in so many wrong ways, and it is such cold comfort to think of her
                                       receiving
love not mine   love she no longer resists.

        Healing that will take a very long time . . .

On my morning walk, I bend to find feathers in the grass, note a scrim
of mist on water; redbuds and forsythia, their blossoms opening to bees.

EVENSONG

Today the trees pull away
      from the ferry,
          the rocks retreat,
              the moorings move
—as if the world is drifting
           and I alone am standing still.

Month follows month
as I watch my daughter
          disappear.

Now, the coyotes
      will not know her.
          The owls
will not know her.
      New daffodils, lilies, wild hyacinth
bloom.

The branches she pruned
      have all been burned,
gleaming sap turned to smoke.
          Each night
I name her
      to the water, to the willow,
          to the sleepless stars.

COMING HOME TO THE RIVER

I could say *my river*
like I say *my daughter*

—but still it moves on

always unknowable,
late winter swelled
to high water,

and to come back
—*home*—I left

full-blown spring
on the island,
the city blustering
with blossoms

so that on my last day
near the ocean
a street cleaner came by,

swept up the petals,
those drifts of pink snow

as if beauty, once
fallen, was unseemly—
tenuous and gone.

I must do something with her
ashes. It's nearly a year.

AND ON

For three hundred sixty-five days I have tried to make her
make sense—ripped out every seam, pulled nails,
dug up roots, sanded to bare wood. I have opened-turned-
drained-clawed, gone to sleep praying she would come to me,
waked in disappointment or tears.

I have looked for her in every eagle, heron, hummingbird;
every cardinal, oriole, fox. Each startling blossom. Each bit of color
I did not expect.

My tongue trips over tenses: have/had, is/was, present-or-past
the flip of a coin. Both and neither, my empty hand still my hand, scars
and blue veins, long lifeline and her silver ring.

I have spread the name I gave her—like seed, willed it forward,
supple as wheat fields in wind, a knife that sharpens with use. Our stories,
just mine now—each a shaky bridge, foot traffic only, how many crossings
before it gives way?

I know where I have stored the locks of her hair, what remains
of her muscle and bone. They pull to me from the chest, pull at me
in my chest, a wound she inflicted that afternoon

one year ago
                    —right now—
        a day filled with trillium, trout lilies, blood root. Last year's leaves
rattle in the trees. The creek rushes over itself
                                        to the river,
                                                to the sea.

A PAUSE IN AN ALL-DAY RAIN

—for Hanna Grayce

In the quietest reach of late afternoon,
the light, without warning, dapples and shifts,
finding new leaves in the saucer magnolia
we planted for you last week.
I watch the green bending, here

and here, think perhaps I should give you
the quilt I've tossed over my bed
—it matches your sofa—catch myself
once more. Friday, I had your name
inked into the skin of my inner arm

so I'd be reminded—not of you
but of your absence, would stop reaching
for the phone. Now I want to tell you
I blistered my hand on the stove,
the cat is showing her age—

I've set up a pad and blankets
near my desk. You should know I'm better
with her; more space in the heart perhaps.
Good morning, luv, I say out loud each day
on waking   to whomever   is listening.

AUTHOR'S NOTE

Sometimes language is the rescuer.
—ANNE MICHAELS

When my daughter Hanna ended her life in late April 2017, I was devastated. In the anguish of the days and weeks that followed, I turned to writing. This was not a conscious decision, and I did not write anticipating any particular result. Even though for the previous ten years, my professional life had centered on writing and healing, I had no expectation that my own writing in the throes of grief would provide rescue or refuge, or that it could help me navigate the unimaginable. In fact, quite the opposite was true. I believed there were no words for the weight of loss, disbelief, and confusion I experienced. I felt I had no way to express the suffocating mix of shock and guilt I felt. I simply turned to writing in order to remember. I kept notes to keep sane—it was happening too fast, and there was too much to trust to memory, too much to hold inside. Overwhelmed, exhausted, utterly bereft, I was flooded with images and stories of Hanna, infant to young adult, and I was terrified they—and she—would disappear. She adored monkey bars. She loved to knit. She was a gifted slam poet. She never wore matching socks. She could do a one-armed push-up. She taught her four-year-old self to ride a bike. There were so many things I needed to remember; there were so many things I could not bear to forget.

And so, almost from the start, I poured my grief into writing. It began with a piece I wrote for the memorial service. I called it "Carrying Hanna." It was a story I alone could tell, having carried my daughter from before her birth. Her life was so much more than the way it ended, and I wanted to call to mind the bright intensity of the child, the growing girl, the young woman she had been. I wanted to present, as well, the paradoxes that were Hanna: passionate, generous, spirited, wounded—a complicated and powerful force in the world. And I wanted to talk about mental illness. Hanna had taken her own life; to me, it was (and still is) incomprehensible. But I wanted to say "mental illness" out loud; I wanted to say "suicide" as surely as I would have said "car accident" or "cancer"—for her sake, and for the sake of others. The family and friends gathered around me recognized the comfort I found in writing, and in sharing, my stories of Hanna—the relief I experienced, even then, in putting my love and my loss into words.

And then, as is often the case with a death, the family and friends who came together so immediately and so protectively needed to return to their own lives, and I faced being alone. Before Hanna died, I had been scheduled

81

to attend a mid-May poetry writing workshop at Wintergreen, a retreat center near Kingston, Ontario. Both the director of the center and the workshop facilitator were women I had known for many years; when they learned of Hanna's death, they encouraged me to continue with my plan, promising there would be no expectations and offering a safe space to let unfold whatever I needed to have unfold. I could write, or I could choose not to write. I could speak, or I could choose silence.

And so, only a few weeks after Hanna's death, I dropped my son, Jesse, at the airport and drove the nine hours to Wintergreen, where I was taken in and held by my wise friends. There, in a circle of poets, I began to write poems. Our first writing prompt, which we were to have completed before we arrived, was to create a poem from art. Since toddlerhood, Hanna had been one of my muses, and even before her death I had imagined writing a poem in which she was the Little Mermaid, based on the statue of the Hans Christian Andersen character that looks over the harbor in Copenhagen. I continued with the poem, but now I wrote it as a foreshadowing—the mermaid as a young woman who considers making a terrible trade (which, in the Andersen tale, the mermaid does), and me, as her mother, unable to stop her. It was my first poem for Hanna after her death. During the remainder of the retreat, I wrote about my first Mother's Day without a daughter; about our last visit together; about bringing her ashes home, wrapped in her baptismal blanket. The poems were small and tight; it was as if I could only manage a few words at a time—but they were necessary words. And writing was the only thing I could do with my overwhelming loss.

I wrote through the entire summer—poems about Hanna's life, baby to young adult. I wrote of the joys and the challenges of being her mother. I wrote of the emotional toll of mental illness, my exhausted efforts, my failures and regrets. I struggled to put into words things I had learned about her childhood only long after the fact. In poem after poem, I grappled with the realities of her death; "gun gun gun," I wrote, needing to remind myself of what I simply could not comprehend, needing to face what I wanted with all my heart to deny. I wrote as if my life depended on it. I wrote *because* my life depended on it.

I spent the fall and early winter living through (and reliving memories of) family occasions and yearly events: my October birthday, Thanksgiving, Christmas. Jesse was with me for each. Then, in January, I travelled to Victoria, British Columbia, to begin a delayed sabbatical. I rented a small apartment near the water and joined the poetry community there. The ocean figured prominently in my poems—it seemed an apt metaphor for all that was incomprehensible and never-ending in my quest to create meaning, to find some explanation that would make things make sense. It was also a symbol of impermanence, mirroring the ways I could already feel Hanna slipping away, my own memories fading. I was terrified my beloved daughter would be forgotten. Jesse joined me for Hanna's February birthday; Easter arrived. And then, in mid-April, I headed back to Michigan, to finish out the first grief-year at home. Jesse came out and we planted a magnolia tree. I had Hanna's signature tattooed onto my arm.

My year of writing for Hanna was over. Of course, I kept writing, but the Hanna poems of that first year were finished, and once the year was past, I did not add to the set. I kept notes of where ideas had come from, where and when poems were written and rewritten, and what the process felt like to me as a mother, as a mourner, as a poet. For several months, I let the poems rest, only occasionally reading one or two at public events. Then Hanna's birthday came again and, on that day, that weekend, I laid out all the poems, listening to find the story they told. It was excruciating, but it was comforting as well to view the result of my mourning writing. I could see how the poems themselves changed across the year; I could see how I wrestled with anger, self-blame, sorrow, confusion, doubt, and how, through and under the loss, there was fierce tenderness and abiding love. When I was invited to speak at a local gathering on my experience with poetry as a healing art, I realized how far I had come on my journey. I also recognized that the journey was not—never would be—entirely done.

* * *

I know from years of study, as well as from my background leading workshops, that there are particular aspects of writing in general, and of poetry in particular, that make it well suited to the healing process. The word *trauma* is based on the Greek word for wound, and like a physical wound, emotional, or psychological trauma wounds the survivor. In or after trauma, the world feels chaotic and grief seems bottomless and unending. Memories carry emotional charge, particularly if the loss has been complicated (and nearly all deaths are complicated, particularly the death of a child; particularly a death to suicide). Survivors most often experience a relentless desire to know *why*, to make sense of what seems senseless, to find personal meaning in and through the grief.

It is a challenge for those who grieve to keep living in a world that never does explain why. Yet certain aspects of writing offer a way to begin to live without answers. If trauma is a wound, then writing is a means of debriding and stitching up that wound—or at least of engaging in that process. It does not prevent scarring, but it may allow for healing to start.

As writers, writing allows us to create some order from disorder, to put shock into words, and from there to explore and examine the source of the trauma, as well as the aftermath and results. We can become observers of our own pain; rather than ignoring or invalidating loss, we revisit and review, making space for more complex understandings and eventually beginning to integrate the loss into life going forward.

Through writing, we are able to continue the work of mourning. The burden of the unsayable becomes less heavy and sometimes, in its expression, suffering may be transformed into something that has beauty. Writing can serve as a public testimony or memorial to loss. Writing helps us uncover links to others—past, present, and future. We discover we are not alone. Ultimately, writing can lead to an acknowledgment of change and a deepened connection to what has been lost.

These healing potentials of writing were clear to me as an instructor and workshop facilitator. But after Hanna's death, I learned them from the inside, experienced them in a more personal and profound way. If each grief is its own, and no two grief journeys are exactly alike, then charting the year in poems not only became my way to memorialize Hanna; it also allowed me to record—for myself and others—the depth of the loss and my own agonized and fumbling responses.

The idea that one can write through and to the other side of grief is largely misleading. Not every story ends with resolution and, for many stories, closure is a myth. After loss, it is most often the case that one learns to live with a hole in the heart. One goes on, as it were, in the company of grief.

In my own writing, what I have created is not a full story, nor fully healing. I have documented a grief-year in poems. Writing did not magically bring me through it and did not lead to full acceptance. But it did provide some measure of comfort—one word, one line, one poem at a time. As I laid the pages out on my desk, I was creating a documentary of loss, a year-long elegy to the daughter whom I could not imagine being without. I was creating a record—a trail of pebbles, hieroglyphs carved on the sides of trees—that would show where I had been, that could manifest a depth of grief that mirrored the depth of my love.

I found healing in the beauty of language and poetry. I remember on several occasions sharing with a friend the writing of the day and being comforted. Not happy, but somehow settled—settled because I had untangled a thorny stanza, or worked out a stubborn metaphor, or found a title that did what I wanted it to do. Settled because the word "merciless" transformed a poem's ending, or lines from the poet Theodore Roethke helped me say more than I knew how to say on my own. Settled because I had found in myths—with their life lessons in loss—a structure around which I could build my own poems.

Bit by bit, the memories I had been terrified I would forget found their way, solid and lasting, into poems. The awful "firsts" took new shape as I found language for what were now devastated traditions. As it had been when I wrote for Hanna's memorial, I was telling a story only I could tell, and I found comfort in putting my love and my mourning into words. There was a certain solace in the intensity of emotions I experienced, the connection with Hanna I created through poems. Ours was an uninterrupted year-long conversation; when I wrote, our history was alive again and she was with me, as present as she had ever been.

I did not know at the start what the poems would become. They did not feel like poems; they felt like shards of something that could never be reconstructed. My dreams. My future. My heart. They were my turns in a conversation that had suddenly, horrifically, ended. They were my voice in a void that had once had a name and a shape—that had done yoga and hung posters, had rescued cats and called me her Mama Bear.

The poems are written from a place of unknowing, from inside the process of grief. Most often, grief is written about from the vantage of time and distance. Something has been learned that is shared; reassurance is offered, promising that excruciating pain is not the forever story. But I did not want to write reassurance. I wanted to write about the awful breaking—open and raw; I needed, for my own sake, to convey the contours of unhealed anguish, to explore the heart of unmitigated ache.

I believed (and continue to believe) that writing with such honesty would in some way have value—that it could keep my connection with Hanna alive, that it would give voice to often-unshared aspects of mental illness and bear witness to the tragedy of suicide, and that it might speak in some way to others experiencing their own traumas and loss.

* * *

My Hanna poems—and the writing of them—led me into early healing. They allowed me to learn and experience my daughter in a new way. They were at once a heartbroken lament and an ongoing love song. Across time, they changed: the early grief poems were spare, tight, straightforward, intense; it took everything I could do to muster just a few words. With time, they expanded, loosened, began to breathe.

The poems brought me closer to Hanna. In writing, she and I were still connected as I struggled to find the words—poetic, symbolic, metaphoric, straightforward, hard-hitting, shocking, tender, and always inadequate words

—to speak of attachment and loss. They were an incomplete record of our life together, but they were the best I could do.

The poems brought me closer to myself as well. I became a witness to my own pain. I held in my mind, with deliberate focus and gentle regard, all that could not be changed—my irreversible brokenness and sorrow. I became a companion to myself in the dialogue that writing creates.

The poems also helped produce community. Others—those who had also lost, those who worked with loss, and those who studied losses—were able to relate and connect. My desire going forward is that these grief poems will nurture wider community over time. Since, in the end, we all experience loss, perhaps the poems will continue to create connection and help provide an entry for the grief processes of others. Perhaps the poems may even speak to those who have considered, or who find themselves in circumstances that lead them to consider, self-harm; it is my deepest wish that those individuals will hear in my words the love that may seem to them to be out of reach, and will recognize the heartbreak and devastation that suicide leaves behind.

In the year following Hanna's death, I wrote into worded existence my own sorrow. In the poems, there is no positive resolution; there is no healed happy ending. But each poem represents a day I woke up and chose to move forward. From that, there is a lot to be learned.

ACKNOWLEDGMENTS

In bringing this book forward, I am grateful both to those who supported me as a writer as well as to those who supported me as a person, grieving. In most cases, there is no difference. I will undoubtedly overlook some individuals I ought to have included; a list such as this is inherently incomplete, and for that, I apologize in advance.

In the time immediately after Hanna's death, I was surrounded by the loving care of Melanie Morrison, Carol Mason-Straughan, Roxanne Klauka, Ron May, Scott Harris, April Allison, Chris Root, Marcia Beer, Skip and Claudia Brevis, Casey Breves, Julian Polaris, Lisa Shull Gettings, Lynn Fendler, Kim Van Es, Stephanie Jordan, Twila Konynenbelt, Cynthia Hockett, Marianne Peel, Stephanie Alnot, Cathy Colando, Kathy Swearingen, Jodene Fine, Beth Herbel-Eisenmann, Terry Edwards, Kristi Lowrie, Karen Gray, Mark McCarthy, Lisa Domke, Tracy Weippert, and Jeanne Loh. I was supported as well by dean Bob Floden and many additional administrators, colleagues, staff, and students at Michigan State University, and by Edgewood United Church of Christ, a faith community with room enough for questioning and doubt.

At Wintergreen Studios in Kingston, Ontario, I was encircled by strong women, gifted writers, wise friends: Rena Upitis, Lise Rochefort, Susan Wismer, and the whole group of poets gathered in May 2017.

In Victoria, I was welcomed and embraced by Wendy Donawa and Leah Fowler, Susan Alexander, Daniel Scott and Planet Earth Poetry, the Barber-MacDonald household (Stuart, Jen, Freya, and Kady), Michelle Poirer Brown, Barbara Pelman, Susan Olding, Liz McNally, Mary Ann Moore, Pam Porter, Arlene Paré and Chris Fox, Cynthia Woodman Kerkham, Tina Biello, Alison Goodman, Chelsea Comeau, Jen Selman, Bonnie Nish, and the late Carl Leggo. Pet-sitter Jack Bishop made my time in Victoria possible by taking in Jamie and Jazz while I was away.

When it came to publication, I acknowledge once more the Michigan State University Press, and especially the director, Gabriel Dotto. Thanks as well to the Women's and Gender Studies program at Michigan State for underwriting part of the production of this book.

In particular, I am indebted to Lorna Crozier and to David Pimm, both of whose care has crossed time and contexts—each an exceptional writer, skilled editor, steadfast guide, and treasured friend.

Most profound appreciation for those who knew and loved Hanna through all of her life (or all of theirs), and who have grieved alongside me with their whole hearts: Dad and Carol, Mike and Rachelle, Brandon, and Elayne.

My greatest gratitude is to my son and Hanna's brother, Jesse, for love and for acts of love too numerous to mention, and for walking beside me week after week, month after month, year after year. As Antonio Machado has written, "Traveler, there is no road; you make your own path as you walk. As you walk, you make your own road, and when you look back you see the path you will never travel again." Indeed.

*   *   *

Much of what I have learned about poetry as survival, trauma as wound, and wound as blessing comes from the writings of poet Gregory Orr.

These poems, or versions of these poems, have appeared in the following:

- JOURNALS: "Seaglass," "End of the Motherline," "Instructions for the Friends Who Are Sorting My Daughter's Things This Afternoon" in *Arc Poetry Magazine*; "The Cruelest Month" in *Nimrod International Journal*; "Elephant Ears," "Easter Morning," and "And on" in *Sixfold*.

- ANTHOLOGIES: "The Little Mermaid," "Patient Stone," "First Mother's Day without Her," in *Always with Me: Parents Talk about the Death of a Child*; "Bipolar," "Too Late," in *Voicing Suicide*; "The Fox" in *50/50: Poems & Translations by Women over 50*.

The poem "On Returning from Holland, I Find a Lone Tulip in My Garden," is modelled after the poem "Flame" by C. D. Wright.